Water Sports
Outdoor Adventure Handbook

Hugh McManners

DORLING KINDERSLEY
London • New York • Stuttgart • Moscow

A DORLING KINDERSLEY BOOK

Editor Patricia Grogan **Art Editor** Lesley Betts
Photography Andy Crawford, Gary Ombler, James Jackson
Production Josie Alabaster

Managing Editor Jane Yorke
Managing Art Editor Chris Scollen

Water-sports consultant Keith Jennings

The water-sports adventurers:
George Bailey, Rachel Butterworth,
Nicholas Culligan, Tanneka Ducille, Rachel Rogers,
Darren Whitehead

First published in Great Britain in 1997 by
Dorling Kindersley Limited,
9 Henrietta Street, London WC2E 8PS

Visit us on the World Wide Web at
http://www.dk.com

A CIP catalogue record for this book is available from the British Library

ISBN 0-7513-5502-X

Colour reproduction by Colourscan, Singapore
Printed in Hong Kong by Wing King Tong

Contents

How to use this book

This book contains all the information you need for safe adventures on water. It shows you how to paddle, row, and steer all kinds of craft and is packed full of useful hints, tips, and ideas. Enjoy your water-sports adventures!

Being safe in the water

Water-sports adventures are fun and safe when you are properly prepared. You need to feel confident in the water so that you can cope in any situation. This section shows you how to improve your survival and swimming skills.

Find out how to make a kit bag on page 8.

Learn how to make an emergency float on page 9.

See page 10 for how to stop your snorkel mask from misting up.

Look on page 13 for how to perform a duck-dive.

Underwater adventures

A snorkel, mask, and fins will enable you to snorkel underwater without needing to come up for air. Learn how to snorkel in a swimming pool so that you can have exciting underwater adventures, including swimming through an obstacle course.

Afloat on your raft

All watercraft have the ability to float, or be buoyant. Make a raft from everyday materials to learn how watercraft stay afloat and then make your own paddles to propel and steer the raft. You can also attach a flag with your own special emblem to the raft.

Learn how to punt your raft on page 18.

See page 17 to find out why you need to wear a life jacket or buoyancy aid on the water.

Learn how to capsize safely in a kayak on page 24

See page 27 for how to make a sail on your canoeing day trip.

Paddling, day trips, and rowing

Canoes are paddled and rowing boats are rowed. This section teaches you the differences between these techniques and how to manoeuvre your craft. Instructions on how to launch and moor your craft will help prepare you for a day trip.

Sailing a dinghy

All sailing boats, or dinghies, are moved by the wind. An Optimist dinghy is the simplest kind, and therefore the best one in which to learn the skills of sailing. Always learn how to sail at a boat club recognized by the Royal Yachting Association.

Find out how to tack on page 33.

Discover why you should always set off sailing into the wind on page 32.

Learn how to measure water-depth on page 37.

Find out how to tie a mooring knot on page 39.

Charts and nautical knots

All sailors need to know how to recognize water on special maps called charts. By learning how to read a chart, you can find out the depth of the water and about any underwater obstacles. It is equally important to learn the main nautical knots.

Finding out more

Many people enjoy water sports, so the water is often crowded. You must learn the basic water rules and be considerate. Why not contact the governing body for your preferred activity and join a club recommended by them?

Look up useful terms in the glossary on page 46.

Use the index on page 48 to find everything in this book.

How to use each page

Each page in this book explains everything you need to know for each adventure. The introduction gives you an overview, and the step-by-step instructions show you how to learn, make, and do all the activities.

Knot symbol
You will see this symbol when you need to tie a knot.

Star symbol
This symbol appears next to important safety points.

Direction arrow
The arrow shows the direction in which the wind and craft are moving.

Boxed pictures
The instructions underneath these pictures explain how to make and do the activities.

Locator picture
A picture appears at the top left-hand corner of each page. It sums up what is being covered on the page.

Most pages have a section showing the materials or equipment you will need for your adventure.

The coloured band on each page reminds you which section you are in. This page is in the Paddling, day trips, and rowing *section.*

Boat symbol
This symbol appears next to useful tips.

Hints and tips
Each hints and tips box is packed full of useful information.

Hints and tips boxes have a picture of a boy or girl. Most pages have one of these boxes.

Extra information
At the bottom of most right-hand pages, you will find additional or new information about the subject.

Water confidence

Before you try any water sport, it is very important that you feel confident in the water. Practise swimming 50 m (164 ft), treading water for two minutes, swimming underwater for 30 seconds, and making an emergency float from a pair of light-weight trousers so that you can cope in any situation.

A kit bag is a handy place to keep your water-adventure gear.

Materials for the kit bag

Safety pin

Needle

Thread

Cord

Scissors

Oblong piece of material

Hints and tips

Apart from when swimming and snorkelling, you should always wear a buoyancy aid or life jacket near and on the water.

If your eyes are sensitive, wear goggles to protect them in the water.

Always test your water confidence in a swimming pool.

Dressed for swimming

All you need for swimming adventures is a swimsuit, a pair of waterproof shoes to protect your feet, and a towel.

When you come out of the water, dry yourself with a towel. This will stop you getting cold.

Rinse out your swimsuit each time you wear it to make it last longer.

If you plan to go in and out of the water often, take an extra towel.

Always wear sun block on sunny days, especially when you are in the water.

See page 38 for how to tie a figure-of-eight knot.

Waterproof shoes will protect your feet from rough ground.

How to make a kit bag from an oblong piece of material

Fold the material in half. Fold over the top edge by 3 cm (1 in) and sew it down securely.

Sew up the bottom and one side to make a bag shape. Do not sew up the folded edge.

Attach a safety pin to 1 m (3 ft) of cord. Thread the cord through the folded edge.

Remove the safety pin and tie the two ends of cord together with a figure-of-eight knot.

How to make an emergency float

Practise making a float from a pair of light-weight trousers. This skill will not only improve your water confidence, it will also help you to cope in an emergency.

1 Practise treading water without using your hands so that you feel comfortable when making the float. Soak the trousers in the water and tie a half-hitch knot in the end of each trouser-leg.

2 Hold the trousers open by the waist-band. Take a breath and throw the trousers behind your head. You may bob under the water, so keep holding your breath in case this happens. Kick hard with your legs to keep afloat.

See page 39 for how to tie a half-hitch knot

3 Keep hold of the waist-band in both hands. Throw the trousers up and over your head to catch as much air as possible in the legs. Repeat until the trouser-legs are full of air.

4 Hold the waist band closed together and pull it just below the surface of the water. Rest your chin on your hands and let the float hold you up. You only need to kick your legs very gently now to stay afloat.

You can work for the Amateur Swimming Association (ASA) Rainbow and Water Skills awards to improve your water confidence.

Snorkelling underwater

A snorkle, mask, and fins will enable you to swim underwater like a fish. The snorkel helps you to breathe while underwater, the mask lets you see where you are going, and the fins allow you to glide easily through the water. Always learn how to snorkel in a swimming pool with an experienced adult.

Snorkelling is the perfect way to explore the world underwater.

Equipment

Mask

Snorkel

Fins

Hints and tips

There are two kinds of fin – shoe type fins and adjustable fins. Whichever kind you use, put them on once you are in the water.

Remember, everything seems much larger and closer when you are underwater,

If you have long hair, keep it tied up out of the way.

Getting ready

Before you start snorkelling, make sure your equipment fits you properly.

1 The edge of the mask should form an airtight seal around your face. When breathing in through your nose, a well-fitting mask will stay on without the strap.

2 Pull the strap over your head to help keep the mask in the correct place. Adjust the length of the strap until it feels comfortable.

3 Attach the snorkel to the looped strap on the mask, see right. Bite lightly on the two rubber stumps in the snorkel mouthpiece and put the rubber plate between your teeth and lips.

How to adjust your mask and stop it from misting over

To adjust the length of the strap, pull the tab through the underside of the mask.

When swimming underwater, the mask will mist over. To avoid this, spit into the mask.

Smear the spit over the inside of the mask. Swirl a little water around the mask to clean it.

To keep your snorkel at the correct angle, slide the snorkel through the looped strap on the mask.

Smart breathing

The snorkel tube should lie against one side of your head, close to your temple. Make sure the tube is angled backwards so that it clears the water. Standing in shallow water, try using the snorkel by breathing through your mouth. With practice, you will learn not to breathe out through your nose.

Temple

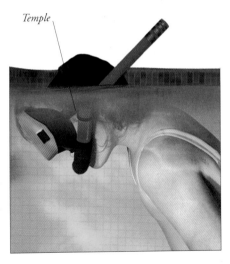

How to clear your mask and snorkel of water

To clear water from your mask, come to the surface first.

Ease the lower-edge seal away from your face and the water will pour out of your mask.

The perfect position

Swimming underwater with fins takes practice. Keep your head down and your arms by your side. Try to keep your legs fairly straight and kick front crawl-style without raising your fins above the surface.

★ Never snorkel alone. Always snorkel with at least two other people.

Practice makes perfect

Moving underwater in fins is called finning. Hold on to the edge of the swimming pool and practise finning. If you can hear your fins breaking the surface, angle your body more.

If your snorkel fills with water, come to the surface and blow out firmly through your mouth.

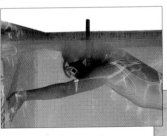

Try to keep your legs as straight as possible and fin from your hips.

⛵ Practise swimming at different depths so that you learn how deep you can go before your snorkel fills with water.

Bend your knees slightly with each kick.

Keep your arms by your side to help you glide through the water efficiently.

Look ahead so that you can see where you are going.

11

With experience, you can dive down to the bottom in your snorkel gear.

Exploring the bottom

When you feel confident snorkelling along the water's surface, you can try snorkelling with your snorkel fully underwater, too. This will enable you to explore riverbeds, shorelines, and lake bottoms. You could also make a snorkel bag to hang around your waist to store your finds in.

Materials for the snorkel bag

Thread

Strip of strong material

Velcro

Needle

Scissors

Oblong of net

String

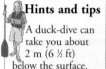

Hints and tips

A duck-dive can take you about 2 m (6 ½ ft) below the surface.

When snorkelling in open water, always wear a life jacket. If you get into difficulty, pull the cord to inflate the life jacket.

Going up and down

Practise holding your breath for one minute and then learn these techniques for moving safely up and down through the water.

Diving feet first

This is the safest way to move down through the water. Keep yourself upright. Point your fins downwards and sweep your arms up above your head to push you down through the water.

A raised arm warns other people that you are surfacing.

Coming back to the surface

As soon as you start to run out of breath, come back to the surface. Tilt your body upwards and raise one hand above your head. As you come up through the water, your raised hand will warn others that you are surfacing.

How to make a snorkel bag to store your finds in

Fold the net in half. Sew up the long edges. Weave cord in and out of one end of the short edges.

Tie a figure-of-eight knot in both ends of the cord. Knot the cord at the bottom of the net.

Weave another piece of cord around the top. Tie this cord to the first cord with a figure-of-eight knot.

Close the top of the bag by pulling the cord tight and securing it with a half-hitch knot.

How to make a belt and attach the snorkel bag to it

Cut about 60 cm (20 in) of material. Sew the hook-side of two Velcro strips to one end of the material.

Sew the eye-side of the Velcro strips to the other end of the material. Space the strips evenly.

Slide the material through the cord on the bag. Wrap the belt around your waist and secure the Velcro.

See page 38 for how to tie a figure-of-eight knot and page 39 for how to tie a half-hitch knot.

Performing a duck-dive

When you have learned to dive feet-first, try duck-diving. You should find this skill easier to perfect than feet-first diving, and you will be able to go deeper in the water, too.

1 Swimming forwards, take a deep breath and prepare to start the dive.

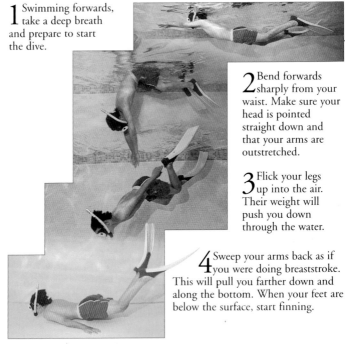

2 Bend forwards sharply from your waist. Make sure your head is pointed straight down and that your arms are outstretched.

3 Flick your legs up into the air. Their weight will push you down through the water.

4 Sweep your arms back as if you were doing breaststroke. This will pull you farther down and along the bottom. When your feet are below the surface, start finning.

Moving along the bottom

Fin underwater for as long as you feel comfortable. As soon as you start to feel short of breath, surface and clear your snorkel. With practice, you will be able to stay underwater for longer periods of time.

Use the Velcro strips to make the belt tighter or looser for comfort.

Set up obstacle course competitions with your friends to test your skills.

Underwater obstacles

Making an underwater obstacle course is the perfect way to develop your snorkelling skills. Once you have made your obstacles, you will need to dive down in the water to position them. This will help you get used to holding your breath, moving up and down through the water, and carrying objects.

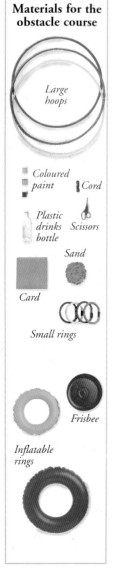

Materials for the obstacle course

Large hoops

Coloured paint *Cord*

Plastic drinks bottle *Scissors*

Sand

Card

Small rings

Frisbee

Inflatable rings

The parts of your course

You can vary your obstacle course depending on what you have at home. However, for safety, never use heavy objects or obstacles in which you could get trapped.

You could ask a friend to time you to see how long it takes to complete the course.

Swimming through a hoop

Always swim slowly and smoothly through a hoop so that you do not hurt yourself. See page 15 for how to weigh down the hoop in the water.

This obstacle will teach you how to fin in a straight line without kicking your legs too far apart.

Inflated rings are useful for adding variety to your course.

Using a marker
You could use a ring as a marker. Raise one hand through the ring before moving on to the next obstacle.

How to weigh down a hoop with a drinks bottle and sand

Pour a little paint inside the drinks bottle. Shake the bottle to cover it in paint. Leave to dry.

Make a cone by rolling one end of the card and sealing it with tape. Fill the bottle with sand.

Get 1 m (3 ft) of cord. Loop the middle of the cord around the bottom of the bottle.

Bring the cord to the top of the bottle and wrap it around the lid. Secure the cord with a reef knot.

Bring the cord around the hoop. Tie the ends of the cord together with another reef knot.

See page 39 for how to tie a reef knot.

Diving for small objects
Combine this obstacle with other parts of your course. You could move a small ring from one obstacle to another or dive down to collect two small objects at a time.

Place small objects on a frisbee and then dive down to collect them.

When you go near water, always wear a buoyancy aid or life jacket.

Building a raft

By building a raft you will understand how a boat floats. A raft is made by tying a platform on to objects that float well, or are buoyant. The raft shown here is easy to make with everyday materials. If you do not have large inner tubes, you could use large airtight containers to make the raft buoyant.

Materials for building the raft

Strong rope

Broomstick

Scissors

Nails

Hammer

Flag

Plastic sheet 2 ½ m (8 ft) square

Trellis 2 m (6 ½ ft) square

Four large inner tubes

Making your raft

This raft will carry two people on a lake. Never take it on open water and make sure an adult is nearby.

1 Arrange the four inner tubes in a square shape. Tie the tubes together with pieces of rope and secure the rope with reef knots.

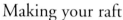
Put half-hitch knots in the ends of the ropes to stop them fraying.

See page 39 for how to tie a reef knot and a half-hitch knot.

You could use a piece of lightweight plywood instead.

2 Lay the trellis over the tops of the inner tubes. Make sure the trellis sits squarely.

The four inner tubes should ideally be larger than the trellis.

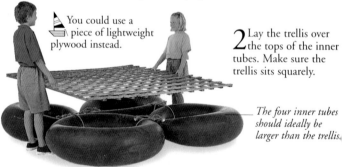

3 Attach the trellis to the inner tubes by wrapping a piece of rope around each inner tube and section of trellis in turn.

Make the rope extra secure by knotting it to the trellis with a reef knot at each section.

Weave the rope through the trellis and pull it tight.

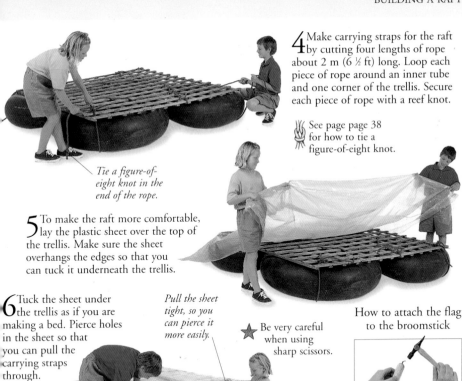

4 Make carrying straps for the raft by cutting four lengths of rope about 2 m (6 ½ ft) long. Loop each piece of rope around an inner tube and one corner of the trellis. Secure each piece of rope with a reef knot.

See page page 38 for how to tie a figure-of-eight knot.

Tie a figure-of-eight knot in the end of the rope.

5 To make the raft more comfortable, lay the plastic sheet over the top of the trellis. Make sure the sheet overhangs the edges so that you can tuck it underneath the trellis.

6 Tuck the sheet under the trellis as if you are making a bed. Pierce holes in the sheet so that you can pull the carrying straps through.

Pull the sheet tight, so you can pierce it more easily.

Be very careful when using sharp scissors.

How to attach the flag to the broomstick

Hammer a nail into the rounded end of the broomstick. Carefully bend the nail over.

7 Finish off the raft by making a flagpole. See right for how to attach the flag to the pole. Secure the pole to the raft with a piece of cord. Wrap the cord around one inner tube and the front of the trellis.

The rope will help keep the sheet in place.

Tie the cord to the pole with a reef knot.

Hook the flag's looped end over the nail and tie the other end to the stick.

Staying afloat

Safety must always come first when you are near the water. If you are a confident swimmer, always wear a buoyancy aid. Nervous swimmers should wear a life jacket, as when in the water, it will make you float on your back.

A buoyancy aid will help keep you afloat in the water.

The large armholes make buoyancy aids comfortable to wear.

The buoyancy on a life jacket is at the front to ensure you float on your back.

Blow through this tube to inflate the life jacket further.

Steering your raft

Floating on a home-made raft is easy and fun. Steering the raft is harder because it has a flat bottom, and it can be blown across the water by the wind. It is important therefore to use your raft only on very calm water. Punting and paddling are the best ways to steer your raft.

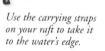

Use the carrying straps on your raft to take it to the water's edge.

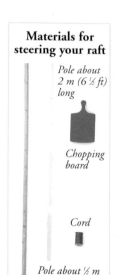

Materials for steering your raft

Pole about 2 m (6 ½ ft) long

Chopping board

Cord

Pole about ½ m (1 ½ ft) long

Pole about 3 m (10 ft) long

Nails

Coloured tape

Hammer

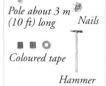

Hints and tips

Decorate your punt pole with strips of the coloured tape.

To paddle forwards, both people must paddle together. If you paddle out of time, you will move around in circles.

Punting your raft

Punting is when you use a long pole to push your raft along. You can only punt in fairly shallow water.

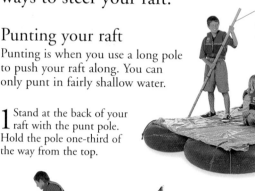

Use the longest pole as your punt pole.

1 Stand at the back of your raft with the punt pole. Hold the pole one-third of the way from the top.

2 Lower the punt pole to the lake bottom. Now push the end of the pole away from you to move the raft forwards.

Twist the pole slightly before you lift it to make sure it does not get stuck on the lake bottom.

3 Bend over and grip the lower end of the pole with one hand. Lift the pole up out of the water, ready to perform the next stroke.

Pivot the pole on your thigh.

4 To steer the raft, use the pole like a rudder. Hold the pole at an angle. Bend your knee slightly and rest the pole against it. Push the pole behind you to steer the raft to the left and in front of you to steer to the right.

18

How to make a paddle with a chopping board and two poles

Make a small loop in one end of the cord and secure it with a figure-of-eight knot.

Use the pole that is 2 m (6 ½ ft) long. Tie the knotted end of the cord to the pole with a reef knot.

The cord should be about 30 cm (1 ft) from the end of the pole. Lay the short end of cord along the pole.

Wrap the cord around the pole until you have covered about 8 cm (3 in) of the pole.

Holding the wrapped cord securely, thread the long end of the cord through the looped end.

See page 38 for how to tie a figure-of-eight knot and page 39 for how to tie a reef knot and half-hitch knot.

Paddling your raft

Once you have made two paddles, try paddling your raft. Kneel on either side of the raft so that it is balanced.

You need two people to paddle the raft.

Kneel down so that you can lean forwards as you paddle.

1 To move forwards, push the paddles through the water from the front to the back of the raft. Lift the paddles out of the water, bring them back to the front and start again.

Put the blade squarely in the water and push it away from you.

2 To turn the raft, sit at opposite corners. The front paddler sweeps the paddle blade through the water in a large arc to the back of the raft. The back paddler uses her paddle as a rudder.

Sweep the paddle to the back of the raft.

3 When both paddles have been pushed through the water as far as possible, the raft will have done a quarter-turn.

Wrap cord at each end of the paddle blade to make it extra secure.

How to make a paddle for your raft (continued)

Secure the cord by threading it through one wrapped piece and tying two half-hitch knots.

Repeat these steps half-way down the pole to make another hand grip for your paddle.

Lay the chopping board over the end of the pole that has no wrapped cord.

Lay the shortest pole over the chopping board and longest pole. Nail all three pieces together.

Secure the paddle blade by wrapping cord around both ends of the two poles. Secure with reef knots.

⭐ If you have not used a hammer before, ask an adult to show you how.

Canoeing with friends

An open canoe can seat at least three people, making it perfect for group adventures. It is usually moved through the water with two paddles – one person paddles at the front, or bow, of the canoe on one side and a second person paddles at the back, or stern, of the canoe on the opposite side.

Open canoes seat several people are the most popular kind of canoe.

Equipment

Paddles

Open canoe

Stepping in

The golden rule for getting into an open canoe is to step in one person at a time.

Always wear a buoyancy aid or life jacket when canoeing.

Sit on the centre of the seat.

Paddle

Blade of paddle

Paddling forwards

You can either sit or kneel in the canoe. Kneeling on one knee will give you more control. Keep your body-weight in the centre of the boat and try not to lean over the side, or gunwale.

See page 21 for how to hold the paddle correctly.

Gunwale   *Grip*   *Shaft*

1 If you are paddling on the right, hold the paddle grip with your left hand and the shaft with your right hand. Do the opposite for the left side. Lean forwards and put the blade squarely in the water.

2 Pull the blade through the water to the back of the canoe. Bend the arm on the paddling side and pull it towards your chest. Your lower arm and back should provide most of the pulling power.

Hints and tips

Keep to the same paddling side. You only swap sides when there is just one paddler in the canoe.

Both paddlers should paddle evenly at the same time to ensure the canoe moves in a straight line.

3 Lift the blade up out of the water and bring it to the front of the boat. You are now ready to perform another stroke. Remember to make sure the blade goes squarely into the water.

How to hold an open canoe paddle correctly

Place the hand opposite your paddling side on the grip. Curl your fingers over the top of the grip.

Wrap the hand on your paddling side around the shaft. Your hands should be shoulder-width apart.

Push forwards with your lower hand and guide the paddle with your upper hand.

Paddling backwards

To paddle backwards in a straight line, make sure both paddlers perform each stroke at the same time.

Remember to look behind you often to see where you are going.

1 Put the blade of the paddle squarely into the water behind you. Twist your body from the hips to give you more pushing power and grip the paddle firmly.

2 Push the paddle through the water as far as you can. Now lift the paddle up out of the water and bring it towards the stern to do the next stroke.

Stopping quickly
Paddle in the opposite direction to stop your canoe. If you are moving forwards, paddle backwards.

About turn

Do a sweep stroke to turn around. Here the canoe is being turned clockwise, or to the right. Do the opposite to turn left.

1 The back paddler puts her blade in the water near the stern and sweeps it in a wide arc to the bow. The front paddler does the opposite.

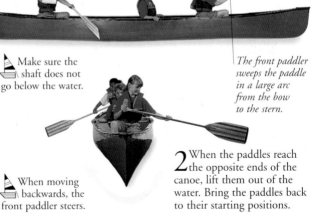

Make sure the shaft does not go below the water.

The front paddler sweeps the paddle in a large arc from the bow to the stern.

Right and left turns
Use the back paddle to steer the canoe when you are moving forwards. To move to your right, push the blade away from you. To move to your left, pull the blade towards you.

When moving backwards, the front paddler steers.

2 When the paddles reach the opposite ends of the canoe, lift them out of the water. Bring the paddles back to their starting positions.

3 Make sure each blade is square to the water and repeat this stroke until you have turned the canoe around.

Kayaking is fun to do with friends, so have a go at your local boat club.

Steering a kayak canoe

A canoe with a closed top is called a kayak. Originally, kayaks were used in very cold or rough water, where open canoes would probably fill with water. Nowadays, kayaks are used on calm water, too. This is the best place to learn to paddle in them, as it takes practice to learn how to balance and steer a kayak.

Equipment

Paddle

Kayak

Getting afloat

To get the kayak into the water, hold the cockpit with both hands. Keep your back straight, bend your legs, and lower the kayak into the water.

★ If the kayak feels too heavy for you, ask an adult to lower it into the water instead.

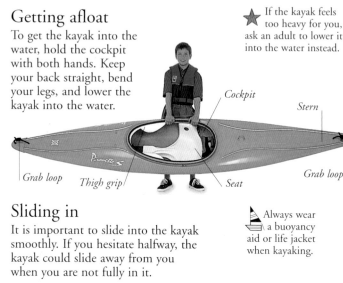

Cockpit

Stern

Grab loop

Grab loop   *Thigh grip*   *Seat*

Sliding in

It is important to slide into the kayak smoothly. If you hesitate halfway, the kayak could slide away from you when you are not fully in it.

⛵ Always wear a buoyancy aid or life jacket when kayaking.

⛵ Place the paddle on the bank within easy reach of the kayak.

Keep your body-weight low.

1 Crouch down and hold the bank with one hand and the back of the cockpit rim with the other. Put one foot into the centre of the cockpit.

Cockpit rim

2 Hold your body-weight with your hands and bring your other leg into the kayak. Straighten your legs and slide them into the kayak. Now quickly, but carefully, sit down.

Keep hold of the bank firmly.

Butt your feet up to the foot rest inside the kayak.

⛵ When seated, open your legs so that they rest on the thigh grips either side of the kayak.

Hints and tips

⛵ You could ask an adult to hold the kayak close to the water's edge when you first get in.

⛵ Getting out of a kayak is the reverse of getting in.

⛵ Use the grab loops to tow or carry the kayak.

How to work out which hand to twist when you paddle

Use an overhand grip to hold the paddle. Keep your thumbs underneath the shaft.

Grip the shaft firmly with one hand, here the left hand, and loosely with the other.

Twist the shaft with your gripped hand. Now grip and twist with your opposite hand. The hand that grips most comfortably is your control hand.

Using your paddle

The blades of a paddle are at right angles to each other, or feathered, so you need to twist the shaft with one hand during each stroke.

Shaft

Grip the shaft with your hands shoulder-width apart.

Blade

See left for how to choose which hand to twist when paddling.

Paddling forwards

Forwards paddling needs some practice to go in a straight line.

1 Reach forwards from the hips with the left-hand blade. Keep your body-weight central and put the blade squarely in the water.

The blade should be fully in the water.

Here, the left hand is the control hand.

2 Keep the blade alongside, or parallel, to the kayak and pull it through the water to the back of the kayak.

3 Lift the blade out of the water. Twist the shaft with the control hand, so the right-hand blade is square to the water. Lean forwards with the right-hand blade and do a stroke on this side in exactly the same way.

Paddle evenly on both sides to move forwards in a straight line.

Paddling backwards

This stroke is the opposite of paddling forwards but a little harder to perfect. You need to twist your body more and look behind you regularly to check where you are going.

1 Twist from your hips and put the right-hand blade squarely in the water behind you. Push the blade towards the front of the kayak.

2 Lift the right-hand blade out of the water and twist the shaft with your control hand, so the left-hand blade is square to the water. You are now ready to put this blade in the water at the back of the kayak and perform another stroke.

Guide the left-hand blade with your left hand.

Remember to keep the blade parallel to the kayak.

Kayak adventures

Kayaks come in many shapes and sizes, each suited for a different activity or adventure. White-water kayaks are long and thin and canoe polo kayaks are short with rounded ends. Despite these differences, all kayaks are long and narrow, making them quite easy to overturn, or capsize.

When you first start kayaking, you will use a general purpose kayak.

Capsizing a kayak

One of the first skills to learn is capsizing safely in a kayak. This is best done in a swimming pool with a qualified instructor.

Always wear a buoyancy aid or life jacket, even when in a swimming pool.

1 Give your paddle to the instructor. Prepare yourself for the capsize by taking a deep breath and pressing firmly on the thigh grips.

2 Grip the sides of the kayak with your arms and lean over to one side. The kayak will then capsize.

3 Wait until you are completely upside-down in the water before trying to get out. Tap the underside of the kayak three times then put your hands either side of the cockpit rim, close to your hips.

4 Keeping your legs straight, lift your bottom and push yourself forwards out of the kayak. Make sure you keep your head tucked in.

Tap the bottom of the kayak before getting out to show you feel confident and that you have not been injured during the capsize.

5 As you leave the cockpit, gently roll forwards. Once you are completely out, swim to the surface. Hold a grab loop and tow the capsized kayak to the pool side. Once you are out of the pool the instructor will help you empty the kayak of water.

Turning your kayak

The final skill you need to master early on is turning your kayak. The easiest way to do this is by performing a sweep stroke.

1 To turn the kayak anti-clockwise, lean forwards from your hips and put the right-hand blade squarely in the water. Push down on your right foot to help with the stroke.

Try to keep your body-weight central rather than leaning to one side.

2 With the paddle just below the water's surface, sweep it in a wide arc from the front to the back of the kayak. Twist your shoulders around with your hips and try to keep your sweeping arm straight.

To turn clockwise, the right-hand blade sweeps from back to front, and the left-hand blade sweeps from front to back.

Keep the blade square in the water.

3 When the blade is as close to the back as possible, lift it out of the water. Twist the shaft with your control hand so that the left-hand blade is square to the water.

Push down with your left foot when sweeping with the left-hand blade.

4 Put the left-hand blade in the water at the back and sweep it around to the front in a wide arc. Repeat this process until your kayak has turned.

Hints and tips

Always tow your kayak upside-down. If you try to turn it the right way up in the water, it will fill with water and may sink.

Kayak slalom racing involves weaving in and out of a series of obstacles as fast as you can paddle.

The course of a kayak marathon can be as long as 193 km (120 miles)!

Different kinds of kayak

Kayak activities are so varied that everyone will find something they enjoy. Once you have mastered your skills in a general-purpose kayak, you could try slalom racing or even surf kayaking!

A sea kayak is long and thin so that you can cut through waves easily quickly without capsizing.

General-purpose kayak

Stunt kayak

Swimming pool kayak

Sea kayak

Planning a canoeing trip

Having learned how to canoe, you could go on a canoeing day trip with your local boat club. Planning is the key to any successful trip. Your canoeing instructor should plan your route and check your canoe and paddle are in good condition. It is up to you to ensure you pack your kit and provisions.

You can go on a day trip in either a kayak canoe or an open canoe.

Materials to waterproof your kit

String

Cord

Plastic bag

Bin liner

🛶 Hints and tips

Tying your kit to the kayak keeps it in place. It also stops you losing your kit if you capsize.

If your kayak has a single piece of string, rather than a securing loop, tie your kit to it with a sheet bend knot. See page 41 for how to tie a sheet bend knot.

Always wear plenty of sun block on hot days.

Being prepared

Pack these items to make sure you are prepared for anything.

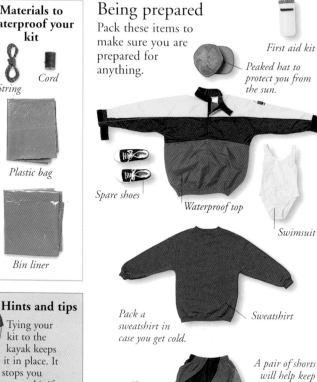

First aid kit

Peaked hat to protect you from the sun.

Spare shoes

Waterproof top

Swimsuit

Pack a sweatshirt in case you get cold.

Sweatshirt

Shorts

A pair of shorts will help keep you cool on a hot day.

Towel

Jogging bottoms

You could pack warm light-weight trousers instead of jogging bottoms.

How to waterproof your clothes and attach them to your kayak

Put your clothes in a plastic bag. Roll the bag and clothes, pushing out any extra air in the bag.

Seal the plastic bag by tying a knot in it. A half-hitch knot will be the easiest one to tie.

Tie 50 cm (1 ½ ft) of string around the knotted bag. Secure the string with a reef knot.

Wrap the string around the bag to keep it tightly rolled so that it will fit inside the kayak easily.

How to waterproof your clothes continued

Slide the bag down the side of the kayak cockpit. Tuck one end of the bag under the seat.

Tie the string on the bag to the securing loop on the kayak with a round turn and two half-hitches.

See page 39 for how to tie a reef knot and a round turn and two half-hitches.

Your packed lunch

Paddling a canoe all day can be tiring and will certainly make you hungry, so always take a packed lunch. Choose food that is easy to carry and that will not spoil if it is a warm day.

Keep your food fresh and waterproof by packing it in an airtight container.

Fruit is very refreshing and easy to carry.

Crisps are a tasty way to end your meal.

Sandwiches are filling and easy to pack.

Always take plenty to drink.

A chocolate bar is full of sugar, which will give you energy.

Packing your kit

Whatever you take with you will be stored in your canoe. This will make the craft heavier and harder to paddle, so only pack what you really need.

Store your kit as close to the cockpit as possible.

Storage space either side of the cockpit.

This kayak has storage space either side of the cockpit.

Buoyancy block

Buoyancy block helps keep the kayak afloat.

Making a sail

If you set off in an open canoe, pack a large bin liner and some string to make a sail. Follow the instructions below for making a sail. You can then sit back and let the wind blow you along for part of your trip.

Hold the sail close to the lashed section.

See page 41 for how to tie shear lashing.

If you have a spare paddle, you can use it as a rudder.

1 Take the two paddles. Tie, or lash, them together firmly with shear lashing along the shaft of the paddle.

2 Pull the ends of the paddles apart to form a cross shape. This cross should be large enough to fill the bin liner.

3 Pull the bin liner over the crossed paddles to make the sail. Kneeling in the middle of the canoe, hold the sail upright.

Rowing a boat

Learning to row a boat takes a little practice because you row facing backwards. This means that each manoeuvre is always the opposite of what you would expect to do. When you first start rowing, concentrate on performing each stroke smoothly and look behind you often to see where you are going.

A rowing boat seats up to three people, so you can take it in turns to row.

Equipment

Oars

Rowing boat

Setting off

Make sure that the rowing boat is tied up, or moored. Step into the boat from the moored end gripping both sides of the boat for balance.

Step into the centre of the boat.

Rowing forwards

You move a rowing boat by rowing with a pair of oars. To go forwards, face the stern of the boat and push it forwards with the oars.

Sit squarely on the centre seat.

Keep the oars close to the side of the boat.

Oars and rowlocks
The rowlock on the side of the boat helps keep the oar in the right position for rowing.

1 Put the blade of each oar in the water behind you, towards the bow of the boat. Lean forwards from your hips and bring your arms straight out in front of you.

Hints and tips

The front of a boat is its pointed end, which is called the bow.

The back of a boat is called the stern.

Always get in and out of the boat one person at a time.

Holding the oars
The end of each oar has a specially shaped hand grip. Hold the oars with an overhand grip.

Imagine the oars are moving in a circle parallel to the side of the boat.

Keep your back straight.

Bring your hands close to your chest.

2 Bend your arms and pull them up towards you. This will bring the blades of the oars through the water to the centre of the boat.

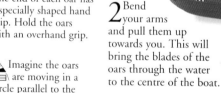

The thin edge of the blade should be alongside, or parallel to, the boat.

3 Lift the oars up out of the water. Sweep them towards the bow of the boat. You are now ready to start a new stroke.

Steering your boat

When you turn your boat, imagine you are using the oars to push and pull it through the water.

You will need to perform this stroke about four times to make a full turn.

1 To move the boat to your right point the blade of your right-hand oar towards the stern, and the blade of your left-hand oar to the bow.

Slide the thin side of the blade into the water first.

Try to stay seated in the centre of the boat.

2 Move the oars through the water. Push the right-hand oar away from you, and pull the left-hand oar towards you.

Keep the blade square in the water, so you have as much pushing and pulling power as possible.

Twist your body from the hips.

3 By now the boat will have turned slightly. Lift the oars parallel to the side of the boat, ready to sweep them across the top of the water.

Make sure the flat edge of the blade is at right angles to the boat. This will make it easier to put the blade back in the water.

4 Bring the oars to the opposite ends of the boat – the right-hand blade pointing to the stern, and the left-hand blade pointing to the bow. Put the blades back in the water and perform the next stroke.

Mooring a rowing boat

When you have finished using your boat, always remember to tie it up, or moor it. The rope that you moor the boat with is called a painter line. Tie this rope to a secure object, such as a mooring ring or post.

See page 39 for how to tie a round turn and two half-hitches.

The painter line is attached to the boat with a figure-of-eight knot.

Place the handle-ends of the oars inside the boat.

Tie this end of the painter line to a secure object with a round turn and two half-hitches.

What is an Optimist?

An Optimist is so easy to sail, you can go out on your own.

A small sailing boat is called a dinghy. There are many different kinds of dinghy, but the Optimist dinghy is the simplest and easiest to learn to sail in. An Optimist can be operated by one or two people and has all the basic equipment of a larger and more complicated dinghy.

The parts of a dinghy

All dinghies have certain features in common. Study the dinghies shown here to learn the names of the different parts.

Always wear a buoyancy aid or life jacket when in the dinghy.

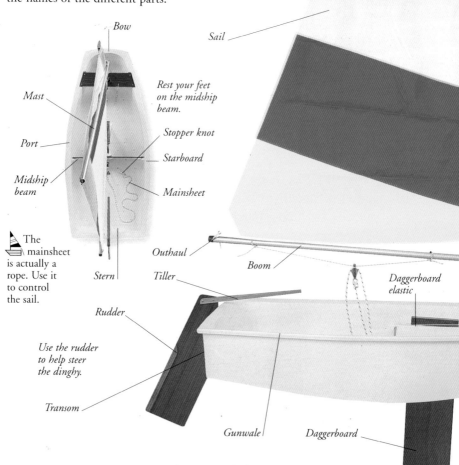

Bow

Sail

Mast

Rest your feet on the midship beam.

Port

Stopper knot

Starboard

Midship beam

Mainsheet

The mainsheet is actually a rope. Use it to control the sail.

Outhaul

Boom

Daggerboard elastic

Stern

Tiller

Rudder

Use the rudder to help steer the dinghy.

Transom

Gunwale

Daggerboard

Preparing to set sail

The easiest way to get into a dinghy is from
a bank. However, if you set sail in shallow
water you will need to push the dinghy out
into the water on a trolley, making sure the
daggerboard and rudder are in the dinghy.
Once in deep enough water, you can push
the dinghy off the trolley and get in.

Four important checks
to carry out before
you set sail

1 When you are on a bank,
get into the dinghy from
the stern or side – whichever
is closest to the bank. Hold
the tiller in one hand and the
gunwale with the other. Step
into the centre of the boat.

Make sure the sprit is
pulled up tightly in the
v-shaped sprit adjuster,
which is on the mast.

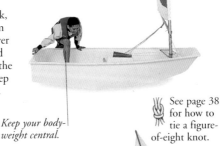

*Keep your body-
weight central.*

See page 38
for how to
tie a figure-
of-eight knot.

The mainsheet should
have a stopper knot tied
in it. This knot is usually
a figure-of-eight.

2 If the dinghy was on a trolley,
push the daggerboard into its
case and clip the rudder to the
transom. Carry out the four sailing
checks shown on the right. Sit to
one side in the stern and hold
the tiller in one hand and the
mainsheet in the other.

Sprit

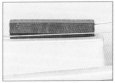

Once in the dinghy,
make sure the dagger-
board is slotted into
place with its elastic.

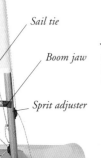

Sail tie

Boom jaw

Sprit adjuster

When you first
start sailing,
always set sail with a
light wind blowing
towards you.

Check the rudder is
properly and securely
clipped to the transom
at the stern of the dinghy.

*Look up at
the sail.*

Use the mainsheet
to let the sail out
and pull the sail in.

3 You are now ready
to set sail. Pull the
mainsheet in so that the
sail fills out and push the
tiller away from you. You
should now move off.

*The daggerboard
helps stop the
dinghy drifting
sideways.*

Sailing upwind

When you first start sailing, make sure there is an onshore wind, and start sailing upwind. If you get into trouble you can then let go of everything in the dinghy and be blown back to land.

When you sail upwind, you are sailing into the wind.

The sail is about 45° to the wind.

When you are facing directly into the wind, the sail will flap loosely.

2 To move the dinghy straight ahead, you will need to turn it. Push the tiller away from you and start pulling in the mainsheet. You are now sailing as close to the wind as you can. This is called beating.

3 If you carry on beating, you will sail forwards but will still move to the side. To go straight on, duck down and pull the mainsheet towards you. The boom will cross over to the other side of the dinghy.

When you are beating with the wind on the port side, you are doing a port beat.

Swapping sides in the dinghy is called tacking.

The sail is now swinging to the port side.

Let the sail fill out with the wind.

Prepare to duck under the boom.

4 Once the boom has swung to the other side, sit down on the opposite side. Swap your hands over on the tiller and mainsheet. Start to pull in the mainsheet and straighten the tiller.

Hints and tips

When the wind blows towards the land, it is called an onshore wind.

A tack also describes the direction, or line, the dinghy is travelling. In step one, the dinghy is reaching on a port tack, and in step five it is on a starboard tack.

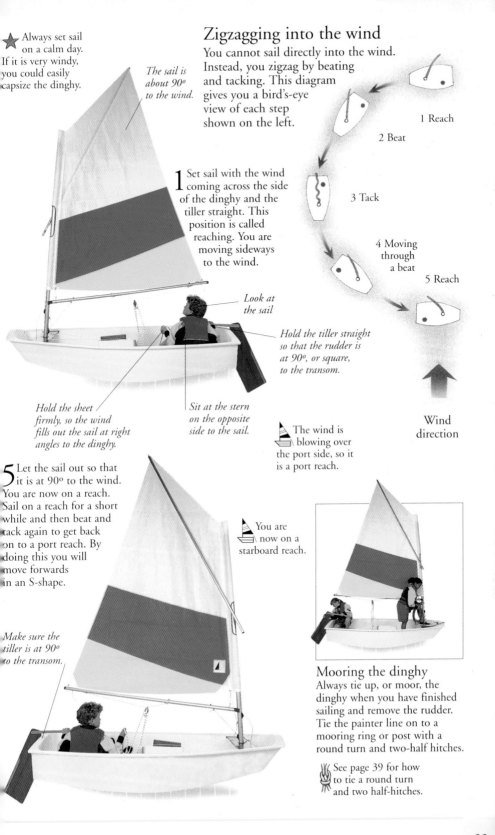

★ Always set sail on a calm day. If it is very windy, you could easily capsize the dinghy.

Zigzagging into the wind

You cannot sail directly into the wind. Instead, you zigzag by beating and tacking. This diagram gives you a bird's-eye view of each step shown on the left.

1 Reach

2 Beat

3 Tack

4 Moving through a beat

5 Reach

The sail is about 90° to the wind.

1 Set sail with the wind coming across the side of the dinghy and the tiller straight. This position is called reaching. You are moving sideways to the wind.

Look at the sail

Hold the tiller straight so that the rudder is at 90°, or square, to the transom.

Hold the sheet firmly, so the wind fills out the sail at right angles to the dinghy.

Sit at the stern on the opposite side to the sail.

⛵ The wind is blowing over the port side, so it is a port reach.

Wind direction

5 Let the sail out so that it is at 90° to the wind. You are now on a reach. Sail on a reach for a short while and then beat and tack again to get back on to a port reach. By doing this you will move forwards in an S-shape.

Make sure the tiller is at 90° to the transom.

⛵ You are now on a starboard reach.

Mooring the dinghy

Always tie up, or moor, the dinghy when you have finished sailing and remove the rudder. Tie the painter line on to a mooring ring or post with a round turn and two-half hitches.

See page 39 for how to tie a round turn and two half-hitches.

Sailing downwind

Moving downwind is easier than sailing upwind. The quickest way to turn around after sailing upwind is by performing a gybe. Having done this, you can sail downwind back to land by running.

You should only ever sail in light winds, especially when gybing.

Turning away from the wind

With the wind behind you and the sail out at 90°, you will be running straight back to land. This diagram gives you a bird's-eye view of each step shown on the right to steer into this position.

6 Running

5 Finishing the gybe

4 Gybing

3 Preparing to gybe

2 Run

1 Reach

Wind direction

4 Pull the tiller all the way towards you. This will make the sail swing over to the other side of the dinghy.

3 To turn the dinghy back to the land, prepare to gybe. Duck down, ready to move under the boom. Start bringing the tiller gently towards you.

Keep your head down.

Keep hold of the mainsheet.

You are now ready to perform a gybe.

2 When the sail is out at 90° to the wind and the tiller is pulled slightly towards you, you will be on a run.

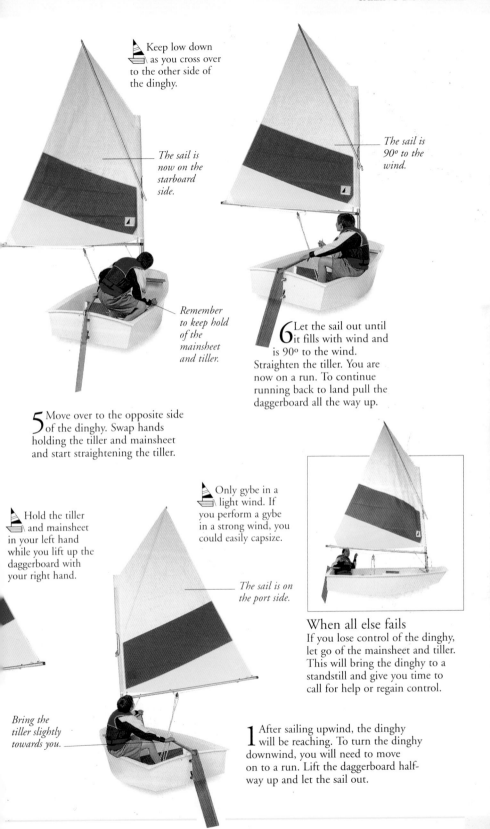

Keep low down as you cross over to the other side of the dinghy.

The sail is now on the starboard side.

The sail is 90° to the wind.

Remember to keep hold of the mainsheet and tiller.

6 Let the sail out until it fills with wind and is 90° to the wind. Straighten the tiller. You are now on a run. To continue running back to land pull the daggerboard all the way up.

5 Move over to the opposite side of the dinghy. Swap hands holding the tiller and mainsheet and start straightening the tiller.

Hold the tiller and mainsheet in your left hand while you lift up the daggerboard with your right hand.

Only gybe in a light wind. If you perform a gybe in a strong wind, you could easily capsize.

The sail is on the port side.

When all else fails
If you lose control of the dinghy, let go of the mainsheet and tiller. This will bring the dinghy to a standstill and give you time to call for help or regain control.

Bring the tiller slightly towards you.

1 After sailing upwind, the dinghy will be reaching. To turn the dinghy downwind, you will need to move on to a run. Lift the daggerboard half-way up and let the sail out.

35

Maps and charts

It is important to know the depth of the water, so you do not run aground.

When planning a day trip, you must have a good knowledge of the area. Large boat sailors often use a kind of map called a chart to gain this knowledge. A chart shows the depth of the water, any underwater hazards, and navigation points. Small boat sailors, however, only need a map to refer to.

Materials for the bag of shot

Elastic band

Scissors

Pebbles

Square of material

Plastic bags

Rope

Hints and tips

The legend tells you what all the symbols on the map represent.

When you give a grid reference, write down the easting number that is on the left of the point first, and then the northing that is below the point.

Legend

▬▬	*Major road*
▭	*Minor road*
⋊	*Bridge*
☁	*Lake*
⬭	*Reservoir*
∼	*River*
⬆	*Forest*
⋎	*Marsh*
—200—	*Contour line*

0–50 m
50–100 m
100–150 m
150–200 m
Over 200 m

Water-depth bands

The north point shows you where north is on the map.

Many lakes have facilities for sailing.

The marsh symbols indicate that you will not be able to launch a craft here.

Contour lines show you the height of the land and the depth of the water.

Underwater contour lines show the depth below sea level.

The depth of the water is shown as blocks of colour on this map. This allows you to see changes in water-depth at a glance.

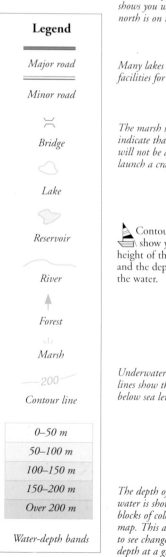

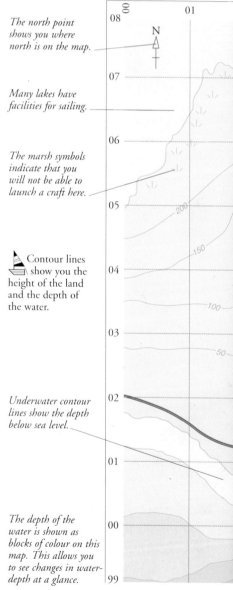

How to read a map

A map gives you all the information that a small boat sailor needs to plan a day trip. It has a legend to explain the symbols, contour lines to indicate the height of the land, and a north point to show you where north is on the map. This map also shows you the depth of the water.

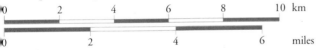

Scale bar

Everything on a map is scaled down and drawn to a fraction of its real size. On this map the scale is 1:50,000. This means that 2 cm on the map is equal to 1 km on the ground.

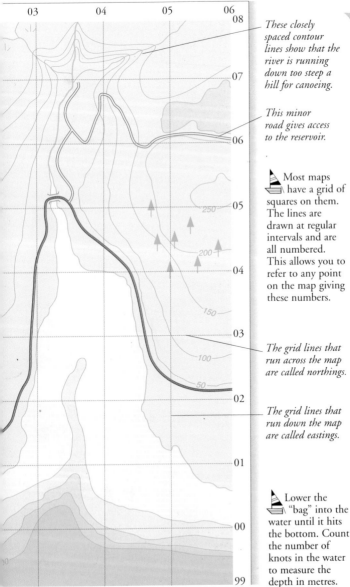

These closely spaced contour lines show that the river is running down too steep a hill for canoeing.

This minor road gives access to the reservoir.

Most maps have a grid of squares on them. The lines are drawn at regular intervals and are all numbered. This allows you to refer to any point on the map giving these numbers.

The grid lines that run across the map are called northings.

The grid lines that run down the map are called eastings.

Lower the "bag" into the water until it hits the bottom. Count the number of knots in the water to measure the depth in metres.

How to make a bag of shot to measure the depth of the water

Put two handfuls of pebbles on the material. Wrap the material around the pebbles.

Secure the material around the pebbles with an elastic band. You now have a bag of shot.

Put the shot in a plastic bag and seal the bag with an elastic band. Place this bag in a second bag.

The shot is now water-proof. Tie the rope to the handles of both plastic bags with a reef knot.

Tie figure-of-eight knots in the rope at 1-m (3-ft) intervals. This rope will measure the water depth.

See page 39 for how to tie a reef knot and page 38 for how to tie a figure-of-eight knot.

Useful nautical knots I

You must always check that all the knots on your dinghy are tied correctly.

There are many different kinds of boating, or nautical, knot, each with a specific use. It is just as important to learn the uses and strengths of particular knots as it is to know how to tie them correctly. For example, a round turn and two half-hitches jams under strain, so it is a very good mooring knot.

Materials

Ropes of varying thickness

Hints and tips

Tying a double figure-of-eight knot is a very quick way to put a loop in a piece of rope.

To stop a natural-fibre rope from fraying, tie a half-hitch knot in the end.

An artificial-fibre rope will not rot as easily as a natural-fibre rope.

A natural-fibre rope is easier to handle than an artificial-fibre rope when it is wet and icy.

Tying a figure-of-eight knot

This knot enlarges the end of a rope. It stops the end running through a ring or pulley.

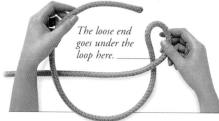

The loose end goes under the loop here.

1 Imagine one end of the rope is attached to a sail. Make a loop with the loose end of rope. Bring this end under and over the loop.

2 Bring the loose end through the loop. Hold the attached end of the rope in one hand to keep the loop secure.

3 Pull both ends of the rope to tighten the knot. Whenever you go sailing, make sure the ends of all the sheets have a figure-of-eight knot.

How to tie a double figure-of-eight knot in a piece of rope

Double-over a piece of rope. Make a loop wherever you want it to be in the rope.

Wrap the looped end of rope up and around the loose ends in a figure-of-eight shape.

Bring the looped end down through the lowest loop in the figure-of-eight shape.

Pull the ends tight. You now have a very secure loop in the end of your rope.

How to tie a half-hitch knot in a piece of string or rope

Use this knot to tie up loose ends. Start by making a medium-sized loop in the rope.

Wrap the right-hand side of the rope around to the back of the loop and then through the loop.

Pull both ends of the rope tight to secure the knot. This knot is used to start many other knots.

Tying a mooring knot

A round turn and two half-hitches is the most common mooring knot. It is a very quick knot to tie and untie.

Right-hand end

1 Wrap the rope twice through a mooring ring or around a post. Bring the right-hand end of the rope under the left-hand end.

2 Loop the right-hand end through the left-hand end to secure the two round turns you have just made.

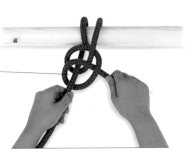

Tie half-hitch knots around this end of the rope.

3 Tie two half-hitch knots in the rope. See the instructions above for how to tie half-hitch knots.

The half-hitch knots should be as close to the round turns as possible.

4 Finish off the knot by pulling the loose end tight and pushing the half-hitch knots close together.

Loose end

⭐ Seal a synthetic-fibre rope by melting the end with a match. Always ask an adult to help you do this.

⛵ A reef knot is a firm, flat knot that will not slip even when it is wet.

How to tie a reef knot with two pieces of rope of equal thickness

Get two pieces of rope. Bring the red piece of rope over and under the yellow piece of rope.

Bring the red piece of rope on the left over the yellow piece of rope on the right.

Tuck the red piece of rope under the yellow piece of rope. Pull on both pieces to secure the knot.

It is very easy to undo this knot. You just push the two ends of rope towards each other.

Useful nautical knots II

Any fastening or loop made in string or rope is generally known as a knot. However, knots can be divided into smaller more specific groups. A bend for example, is a knot that is used to tie two pieces of rope together. A lashing is another kind of knot, used to join poles and other long objects together.

Always keep extra lengths of rope tidy by coiling them into neat loops.

Materials

Rope

Cord

String

Hints and tips

Make sure that any rope you use is not damaged, as it could easily break under pressure.

Most modern ropes are made of nylon or polyester.

Practise tying each knot at home so that you can tie any knot quickly when you need it.

Most ropes are made of three strands plaited or braided together.

Tying a bowline knot

This is the most commonly used knot for making a loop. It will not slip or tighten, making it a very safe loop.

1 Decide how big you want the finished loop to be as you cannot change its size once the knot is tied. Make a small over-hand loop and bring the end back up.

End of rope (the rabbit)

Think of the end as a rabbit coming out of its hole (the loop).

The amount of rope at this end determines how big the finished loop will be.

2 Pull the end of the rope up through the over-hand loop you have just made.

Held end of rope (the tree)

3 Bring the end of the rope around the back of the held end of rope. Now bring the end round to the front and down through the loop.

Pull this end of the rope.

Imagine the rabbit goes around the tree and back into the hole.

4 To finish the knot, pull the held end of the rope. This will secure the loop. You can also use this knot to fasten a sheet to a sail.

How to join two ropes of unequal thickness by tying a sheet bend knot

Make a loop in the thickest piece of rope. Now slide the thinner piece of rope through it.

Bring the thin, blue rope around the back of the thicker, looped, yellow rope.

Tuck the end of the blue rope underneath the part of it that crosses the looped, yellow rope.

Pull the end of the blue rope tight. The two pieces of rope are now securely fastened together.

★ Once you have tied a knot in a piece of rope or string, its strength will be halved.

⛵ If you use artificial-fibre rope on a dinghy, you will need to wash the rope regularly to remove any grit.

Tying shear lashing

Shear lashing is a good way to join together long objects that are parallel, or alongside, each other.

1 Here, we are joining two paddles. You will need about 2 m (6 ½ ft) of string. Make a loop in one end of the string and lie it along the top of one of the paddles.

Short end

3 Bring the string through the loop you made at the beginning. Press the wrapped string firmly against the paddles.

Top end

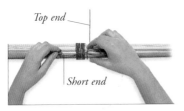

Short end

5 Bring the two ends of the string around to the front of one of the paddles. Push the wrapped string together and keep the loops tight.

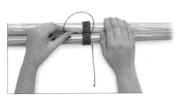

7 Join the two ends together by tying a reef knot. See page 39 for how to tie a reef knot. This kind of lashing is very useful if you want to pull the two objects apart to make an A-frame shape.

This loop is about 8 cm (3 in) long.

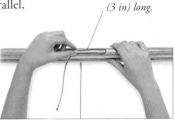

2 Hold the short end of the string firmly in place and wrap the long end of string around the two paddles about ten times.

4 Hold the top end of the string firmly and pull the short end. This will close up the loop and secure the top end of the string.

6 Bring one end of the string over to the other side of the wrapped string. Now thread it between the two paddles and around the wrapped string several times. Repeat with the other end of string.

First aid

When carried out with care, most water adventures are very safe. However, it is important to know basic first aid so that you can cope confidently and quickly in an emergency. Always take a first aid kit with you, and make sure you know how to use all the items in it.

Make your first aid kit waterproof by sealing it in an airtight container.

First aid kit

Waterproof plasters to protect cuts and grazes.

Tape to secure gauze bandages.

Tweezers to remove insect stings.

Safety pins for securing slings.

Calamine cream to soothe sunburned skin.

Gauze pad to treat cuts and grazes.

Scissors to cut plasters.

Triangular bandage for tying an arm sling.

Changing temperatures

When you are outside, your body is more sensitive to changes in the temperature. You need to know what to do if you get too hot or too cold.

Calamine lotion soothes sunburned skin.

Too much sun

If you have been in the sun too long without suntan lotion, you will get burned. If this happens, move into the shade immediately and apply a soothing cream to the burned skin.

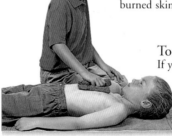

Too much heat

If your body overheats, you may suffer from heatstroke. Move into the shade and remove your outer clothing. Ask a friend to sponge you with cool water until your temperature returns to normal.

Heatstroke will make you feel dizzy and hot.

Not enough sun

If you get very cold and your body temperature falls, you may get hypothermia. This condition can be very dangerous. The most important thing is to heat your body up slowly. Wrap up in warm clothes and blankets, and have a warm drink and some sugary food.

If you feel cold and shivery, get out of the water and warm up straight away.

How to treat a wasp sting with tweezers and a cold compress

Use a pair of tweezers to remove the wasp sting. Hold the injured area to keep it still.

Grasp the sting with the tweezers as close to the skin as possible. Pull the sting out carefully.

Soak a piece of gauze in clean cold water to make a compress. Cool the area with the compress.

⛵ Never grasp the sting at the top as you may squeeze the poison sac.

Treating a blister

Blisters are very common when doing water sports. If you see a blister developing, stop your activity and treat the blister before it gets any bigger.

A kayaking blister

The most common place to develop blisters when kayaking is at the base of each finger.

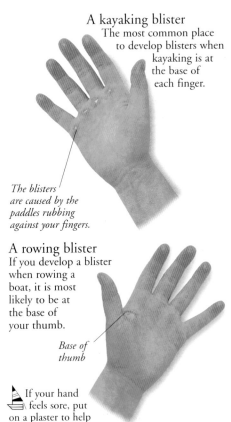

The blisters are caused by the paddles rubbing against your fingers.

A rowing blister

If you develop a blister when rowing a boat, it is most likely to be at the base of your thumb.

Base of thumb

⛵ If your hand feels sore, put on a plaster to help stop a blister forming.

How to clean and protect a blister with gauze and a plaster

Clean the blister thoroughly with soap and water. Now rinse it with clean, warm water.

For several blisters or one large blister, protect the affected area with a piece of clean gauze.

Lay the gauze over the affected area. Secure the gauze by taping it to the patient's skin.

⛵ Protect a small blister with a plaster that has a pad large enough to cover the affected area.

Treating cuts and grazes

When you are in the water, a cut or graze can easily become infected. It is therefore important to protect the affected area with a waterproof plaster.

1 Gently wash the cut or graze with a clean gauze pad soaked in clean water. If you do not have a gauze pad, use cotton wool instead.

2 Try to remove any bits of dirt or gravel. Be very gentle because it may cause a little fresh bleeding.

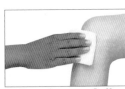

3 Get a clean non-fluffy pad – gauze is ideal. Press the pad firmly over the cut or graze to stop it bleeding.

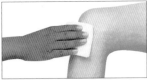

4 Protect the cut or graze with a waterproof plaster. Choose a plaster with a pad large enough to cover the cut or graze.

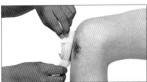

Always wear a buoyancy aid or life jacket on and near the water.

Water rules

The water is often a busy place, especially on sunny days. To make sure that all your water-sports adventures are fun and safe, it is important to remember a few golden rules. When out in a group, always follow the instructions given by the leader and be considerate of other people and animals.

Countryside Code

All adventurers should know the Countryside Code. The points shown on these pages are especially important for water-sports enthusiasts, so make sure you learn them before you set off.

If you pass through a gate on your way to the water, leave it as you found it.

Take any rubbish home or put it in a bin. Rubbish is not just horrible to look at, it can harm wildlife and plants too.

Carry your craft along authorized routes, paths, and slipways to the water's edge.

It is very important to make sure that your craft is in good condition and is properly equipped. Always use equipment from a reputable boat club to ensure that it is safe.

Pack a first aid kit and make sure you know how to use it.

Never go on or near the water alone. You must always go out in a group of at least three people. If someone gets hurt, one person can stay with him or her, while another person can go to get help.

Respect wild animals, particularly during their breeding season and when they are bringing up their young. If you get too close to a swan with her cygnets, she may lash out at you.

Make sure you know how to control your watercraft. If you are on busy water, you may need to manoeuvre out of someone else's way.

Small boats can be manoeuvred much more easily than large boats. If you come across a large boat, always give way to it.

Observe all warning signs. If you do not, you could find yourself dangerously close to water-hazards such as weirs.

If you want to go swimming or snorkelling, find out when and where it is safe to go.

Respect the feelings of the local community. People often live near the water, so do not shout or make a lot of noise. Keep a look out for other groups of people and try not to obstruct their course.

Keep away from banks or other areas where people are fishing. If someone is casting, or throwing a fishing line into the water, wait until he or she has done so before passing.

Always get permission from the landowner before going on private land.

Always launch and moor your craft at an authorized site, such as a jetty.

At the end of every adventure, always remember to moor your watercraft securely to a mooring post or ring.

Glossary

Beat
A sailing position where you sail as close to the wind as possible.

Bow
The front of a canoe, dinghy, or rowing boat.

Buoyancy
The ability to float easily on water.

Buoyancy aid
A vest-style top that is worn to help keep you afloat and safe in the water.

Capsize
When a boat has overturned in the water it has capsized.

Chart
A water map that shows you the depth of the water, any underwater hazards, and landmarks that will help you to find your way, or navigate.

Control hand
The hand that twists the paddle shaft when paddling a kayak.

Daggerboard
A straight board that slots down through the bottom of a dinghy. It helps stop the dinghy

moving sideways in the water.

Duck-dive
A kind of dive used when snorkelling to move down through the water.

Fin
The foot-wear worn when snorkelling. Swimming through the water in fins is called finning.

Gunwale
The upper edge on the hull of a canoe, dinghy, or rowing boat. *It is pronounced gunnel.*

Hull
The main body of a canoe, dinghy, or rowing boat including its sides and bottom.

Kayak
A closed canoe that is usually paddled by one person. *It is pronounced kiyak.*

Leeward
The side towards the wind. On a leeward shore, the wind will be blowing from the water to the shore.

Life jacket
A top that is very buoyant when inflated. In water, a life jacket will keep you afloat on your back with your head out of the water.

Mainsheet
The rope that is used to control the sail on a dinghy.

Moor
To tie up a canoe, dinghy, or rowing boat to a secure point on the land, such as a mooring ring or post.

Port
The left-hand side of a canoe, dinghy, or rowing boat when facing the bow.

Reach
A sailing position where the wind comes from the side of the dinghy.

Rowlock
A horse-shoe shaped attachment found on the gunwale of a rowing boat. It is used to hold the oar in place. *It is pronounced rolock.*

Rudder
The blade found at the stern of a dinghy. It is attached to the tiller and helps steer the dinghy.

Run
A sailing position where the wind is directly behind you and the sail is at right angles to the wind.

Sounding
A measurement that shows the depth of the water. Soundings are recorded on charts.

Starboard
The right-hand side of a canoe, dinghy, or rowing boat when facing the bow.

Stern
The back of a canoe, dinghy, or rowing boat.

Surf kayaking
A sport where you surf over waves in a kayak.

Sweep stroke
A way of turning a canoe or kayak. The blade of the paddle is swept in a large, shallow arc through the water from one end of the canoe or kayak to the other.

Tack
A sailing position where the sail is moving from one side of the dinghy to the other. This position makes the dinghy change its direction. A tack is also used to describe the general direction a dinghy is travelling in.

Tiller
The lever that is attached to the rudder on a dinghy. The tiller is pushed and pulled to move the rudder, which steers the dinghy.

Treading water
A way to stay afloat using as little energy as possible. It is an important water survival technique. Keeping yourself upright in the water, kick down and out with your legs and sweep your arms in front of you breaststroke-style.

Watercraft
A boat of any kind or several boats.

Windward
The side away from the wind. A windward shore will have the wind blowing from the shore to the water.

Useful organizations

British Canoe Union (BCU)
John Dudderidge House
Adbolton Lane
West Bridgford
Nottingham NG2 5AS

Canoe Association of Northern Ireland
Clare Medland
114 Upper Lisburn Road
Finaghy
Belfast BT10 0RH

Scottish Canoe Association
Caledonia House
South Gyle
Edinburgh EH12 9DQ

Welsh Canoeing Association
Pen y Bont
Corwen
Clwyd LL21 0EL

The British Sub-Aqua Club (BSAC)
Telford's Quay
Ellesmere Port
Cheshire L65 4FY

Amateur Rowing Association
6 Lower Hall
Hammersmith
London W6 9DL

Royal Yachting Association (RYA)
RYA House
Romsey Road
Eastleigh
Hampshire SO5 4YA

Royal Yachting Association Scotland
Caledonia House
South Gyle
Edinburgh EH12 9DQ

Amateur Swimming Association (ASA)
Harold Fern House
Derby Square
Loughborough LE11 5AL

Welsh Amateur Swimming Association (WASA)
Wales Empire Pool
Wood Street
Cardiff CF1 1PP

The Scottish Amateur Swimming Association (SASA)
Holm Hills Farm
Greenlees Road
Camburslang
Glasgow G72 8DT

The Irish Amateur Swimming Assocation
The House of Sport
Long Mile Road
Dublin 12

Index

Acknowledgments

Dorling Kindersley would like to thank:

The Islington Boat Club for the use of their equipment while on location; Paul Anderson for his invaluable assistance while on location; Lee Valley Watersports Centre for use of their reservoir; Whitewater The Canoe Centre for lending us the open canoe; Perception Kayaks for lending us the kayaks; Pioneer for lending us the rowing boat; Topper International for lending us the Optimist dinghy; William McManners for lending us his Jolly Roger flag; Sally Hamilton for picture research assistance.
Illustrations: Nick Hewetson

Cartography: Jane Voss, David Roberts
Picture research: Mollie Gillard
Picture credits: T top; B below; C centre; L left; R right; A above; B below
The publisher would like to thank the following for their kind permission to reproduce the photographs: Colorsport 44 CR, 45 TL; Natural Image: Mike Lane 45 TR; PPL: John Nash 45 TC; National Trust Photographic Library: Leo Mason 45 CLB; National Trust Photographic Library: Ian Shaw 45 CRA; Pyranah 25 BR; Sporting Pictures (UK) Ltd 45 CRB.